BEREAVEMENT SUPPORT GROUP PROGRAM FOR CHILDREN
LEADER MANUAL

Beth Haasl, B.S.

and

Jean Marnocha, M.S.W.

 **ACCELERATED DEVELOPMENT INC.**
Publishers
Muncie   Indiana

BEREAVEMENT SUPPORT GROUP PROGRAM FOR CHILDREN

LEADER MANUAL

2 3 4 5 6 7 8 9 10

Printed in the United States of America

Technical Development: Tanya Dalton
                                    Delores Kellogg
                                    Marguerite Mader
                                    Sheila Sheward

ISBN: 1-55959-011-4

ACCELERATED DEVELOPMENT INC., Publishers
3400 Kilgore Avenue
Muncie, IN 47304
(317) 284-7511
Toll Free Order Number 1-800-222-1166

FOREWORD

If you are starting a support group for bereaved children let this manual be the first step of many big steps in the future.

You will find PRACTICAL INFORMATION that will assist you in planning the size of the group, the basic goals and/or objectives of the group, leadership responsibilities, and outlines of each session. This concise information will aide you in all aspects of your endeavor.

You will be exposed to (1) "tips" on choosing the right personality for the leader/facilitator position, (2) helping children with self-esteem issues in their grieving process, and (3) other helpful aids in the development of your children's grief support group.

This manual is not "the answer" to all your questions. However, it will erase many of the major questions you may have. It will help you with the task at hand, helping children with their task of grieving.

Richard J. Obershaw

PREFACE

This manual has come about as a result of our search for materials on methods to help children cope with grief. With the assistance of MSW student intern, Cindy LeClair, the Bellin Hospice Program developed a group program for its grieving children in 1980-81, but was unable to find written materials on grief programs for children. Many books were available on the theoretical aspects of grief in children, but not much was written on the specific "how to" in working with grieving children.

This project led to a cooperative venture between the Bellin Hospice Program and St. Vincent Hospital's Grief Care Program in establishing a children's bereavement group program for the community in 1982. While utilizing the theoretical information on children's grief, much of what we developed was by "trial and error," and learning what activities and what type of group format would work best for children.

As the program developed, other hospice groups and community mental health personnel became interested in the material and requested information on establishing their own group programs. These requests, coupled with the absence of published materials specifically on this topic, led to the writing of this manual. The children's bereavement group program, now solely supported by the Bellin Hospice Program, continues to this day to provide the children of this community with a support system when someone they love has died. It is our hope that other communities will be able to use the information in this manual to benefit their grieving children.

We would like to thank Bellin Hospice for allowing and encouraging the development of this program, Brian Young for the proofreading of our original manuscript, and Andy Haasl for his expertise with the word processor. Thanks also to our husbands, Andy Haasl and John Marnocha, for their continuous support and encouragement throughout the writing process.

Special thanks go the children who have participated in our grief groups since it began, for their willingness to share their personal loss with us. The examples of artwork and writing included in the manual come from them, and they have taught us more about living with loss than we can ever hope to learn by reading about it in books.

CONTENTS

LIST OF FIGURES

PART A
STRUCTURE

1

INTRODUCTION

This manual presents the format for establishing and conducting a *Bereavement Support Group Program for Children*. The five session program is designed for children between the ages of 5 and 15 who have experienced the death of a loved one, or other significant losses. Also included are suggestions on expanding the program, should you so desire.

The information in this manual is based on what we have learned from actual experiences with grieving children and from facilitating bereavement groups for children for the past six years. Since resources available outlining the implementation of a bereavement group program for children are limited, this manual will provide you with information and tools in establishing your own bereavement group for children.

A *Participant Workbook* is available as a supplement to this manual, which contains information on the group sessions, suggested readings, directions, and space to complete all of the activities, all directed towards the children participating in the sessions. This workbook provides each participant with all the materials needed for all sessions, which they may take with them for their review and as a remembrance of the group.

The following information offers a starting point from which you can expand to meet your individual program needs. In beginning a children's bereavement group, a helpful procedure is to gather information and assess community resources before implementation. Facilitating a bereavement group for children can be challenging and intimidating, yet extremely rewarding! The key is to recognize that once you have developed the plan for your program, you must put aside your doubts and begin!

2

RATIONALE

In working with bereaved families what has become apparent is that often available support for the grieving child is lacking. Many adults are uncertain about how children will grieve and about how to be supportive. Adults also may be uncomfortable with their grief because they do not have adequate information about children's grief.

Parents may not be able to be supportive to their grieving children because of their own feelings of grief. Parents are concerned that they may cause their children's grief to worsen by expressing or sharing their own grief. Parents often have difficulty in dealing openly with grief issues as well.

Children may have the same protective attitude toward parents or other adults. They may be reluctant to share their grief with adults who are grieving the same loss because they do not want to upset them.

A bereavement group program such as this is helpful in allowing children to express openly their feelings of grief, and to receive support from others who are grieving. The children learn that other children are experiencing grief and that they are not alone in their feelings.

The program also may be welcomed by parents in that it not only offers opportunity for their children to express their grief, but it tends to promote more open discussions at home concerning the loved one who has died. The group leaders also are able to provide a role model for grieving children in expressing their grief, by providing basic grief information to the children and by talking openly about feelings and issues associated with the grief process.

3

OBJECTIVES

1. **To provide bereaved children with an opportunity to meet in an accepting and safe environment, and to share with other children who have experienced the death of a loved one.**

The chance to meet other children in an informal atmosphere has several benefits for participants. First, it can help to reduce the sense of isolation that the bereaved child may feel just knowing that other children have experienced death and grief. Second, a safe and accepting atmosphere is helpful in encouraging children to share their feelings about grief. Often it is difficult to talk about the death with family members who are also grieving, or with friends who have not experienced a death.

2. **To give bereaved children information on grief in order to facilitate a better understanding and expression of their own feelings.**

Receiving information on the grief process can reassure the bereaved child that his/her feelings of grief are normal. It can help the child to identify feelings about which uncertainty exists, to be more comfortable in expressing them, and to understand the grief responses of family members and friends.

3. **To help children recognize appropriate alternatives in expressing their grief.**

Children can benefit by learning from appropriate role models/facilitators various alternatives for expressing grief. Group discussion, sharing, and the suggested group activities help to offer appropriate ways to cope with grief. By experiencing the program's activities the child has the opportunity to begin working through his/her grief.

4

ESTABLISHING THE GROUP

In beginning to organize a children's grief group, it is important to contact and cooperate with other community agencies that also may be working with grieving children. This becomes more necessary in a smaller community as opposed to a larger metropolitan area, in order to avoid duplication of services available for grieving children. Once you have contacted other community agencies and determined who will facilitate the group, a helpful procedure is to meet with other professionals who are involved with children or children's groups to make them aware of the program and share ideas.

Setting the basic group outline of activities and establishing a timetable is the next step. Many suggested activities follow in Parts B and C.

RECRUITMENT

Developing a brochure can be useful in making others aware of your program. Figure 1 is an example of a brochure briefly outlining and describing the program.

We suggest that the following persons be sent a brochure with a cover letter, providing an introduction to the program: pediatricians, clinics, schools, churches, counseling agencies, boys' and girls' clubs, other bereavement programs, funeral directors, and coroner's offices. In addition to sending information to these agencies, you may need to make presentations explaining the group program at appropriate agency staff meetings.

Bellin
Hospice Program

Life . . .
    Is for the strong
Death . . .
    Is for the stronger.
But facing them both . . .
    Is for the strongest.

Bellin Memorial Hospital

For further information contact:
Bellin Hospice Program
P.O. Box 1700
Green Bay, WI 54305
433-3683

A Program
For Bereaved
Young People

Back of Flyer   **Front of Flyer**

Figure 1. Sample of a brochure describing the program.

Figure 1. Continued.

Bereaved Young People's Group

Grief is a universal emotion—one that can overwhelm the young as well as the old. When a child loses a loved one, there may be feelings of sorrow, loneliness and anger.

To help young people work through grief Bellin Hospice is sponsoring a very special program designed for bereaved children. There will be two alternate groups: one for ages 5-10, and the other for ages 11-15.

The Bereaved Young People's Group will meet once a week for five weeks and will use experiential exercises, artwork, films, speakers, and discussion.

Session I
   An introduction to the program and sharing of life and death attitudes.

Session II
   Feelings and self-esteem

Session III
   How to express memories in a postive way.

Session IV
   Funerals—how they have helped.
   Letter writing.

Session V
   Puppet/role play.
   Ways to share and cope with grief.
   Wrap-up with parents.

Parents are asked to be involved in the initial phase of the program. While parents will not attend the young people's sessions, they will meet at two separate times:

—once prior to the first young people's meeting.

—again at the end of the fifth session.

If parents would like to meet more often, this can be arranged.

The group will be facilitated by Jean Marnocha, Social Worker, and Beth Haasl, Grief Counselor.

This is no charge for participating.

For more information or to register, call Bellin Hospice, 433-3683.

Left Side   **Right Side**

Inside of Flyer

Another way to inform the community about the program is through a story in the local newspaper featuring the children's bereavement group program. Local television stations may also be interested in focusing on the group for their community service programs.

Notification that the program will begin may be done in a variety of ways. For those who have access to a list of recently bereaved persons through a hospital or a hospice program an invitation such as is shown in Figure 2 could be sent.

COMPOSITION

Size

Optimum group size is seven or eight members. Groups have been held with as few as 2 and with as many as 15. It is difficult to predict the number of participants and to regulate the size, as the program needs to be responsive to the needs of the community. To limit the group size and suggest a child wait until the next session or to fail to hold the program due to too few participants, may not meet the child's grieving experience and thus is not suggested.

The program format can be modified to meet the needs of the group size. If the group size is very small (3 to 5), sessions can be consolidated and shortened or decreased to perhaps three sessions. If the group size is large (10 to 15), the group can be divided according to age and maturity levels, and run concurrently by the two group facilitators and perhaps two assistants. One technique for dividing the group is to have certain basic activities in each session completed as a full group, such as sharing the memories, visiting the funeral home, or listing feelings normal to grief. The group then can be separated into the two smaller segments for activities specific to their age group, such as the writing or discussion activities.

Dear Hospice Friends,

The Bellin Hospice Program is offering a children's
Grief Support Program for children from 5-15 years
of age. This program will give children an opportunity to share their grief experience or just
listen to others in the same situation. The dates
for the groups are listed below and a description of
the programs are enclosed.

> CHILDRENS GROUP-The Childrens Group is designed
> for children 5-15 years of age and is facilitated
> by trained group leaders who will provide and oppor-
> tunity to share common grief experiences and learn
> about the grief process. It is not designed as a
> therapy group and you do not need to be having a
> difficult time to participate.

AFTERNOON SESSION

        DATES: February 8, 15, 22, 29 and March 7
                 (Five consecutive Monday afternoons)
        TIME: 4:00 - 5:30 p.m.
        PLACE: Charlotte Fowler Building, Corner Cass
                 and Webster Avenue, Room 112

It is necessary for you to return the enclosed registration
form if interested in attending. Please return registration
form to Bellin Hospice, P.O. Box 1700, Green Bay, WI 54305.

If you have any questions, please call me at Bellin Hospice,
433-3683.

Sincerely,

Beth Haasl
Grief Counselor

rv
enclosure

Figure 2. Sample of an invitation sent to persons who may
want to join the support group.

Age

Five years of age has been an acceptable guideline for the lower age limit. Although their attention span and ability to express themselves is not as developed as school age children, they have usually experienced kindergarten or pre-school, which helps them adapt to a structured experience. If they become disruptive due to lack of attention span, separating them for portions of the sessions or certain activities or providing more individual attention to them in the group may be necessary.

Pre-adolescents through the age of thirteen have shown an interest in attending the group program, with some adolescents through sixteen years old feeling comfortable about attending. If the number of children is sufficient, separate them according to age levels. If the age range in the group is from five through fifteen years, with seven to ten participants, it is workable to conduct the group program as outlined. The older children may assist the younger children as a role model for their grief experience. The younger children can add to the group with their spontaneity, and by asking questions or making statements that the older children may be too embarrassed to ask.

In forming groups, the developmental level of the child is more important than the age. If ideal conditions were possible similar developmental levels would be the group's composition; however, this is not always possible and when not, the facilitators must recognize and work accordingly.

Circumstances of the Death

The mode of death has been varied in the groups conducted, from death by natural circumstances to suicide or homicide, or sudden versus expected death. In the case of suicide, to have more than one child with that experience is helpful so that they know that they are not alone in experiencing the suicide of a loved one; however, doing so is not always possible. The facilitators can point out that many children in other groups have experienced a loss through a suicide.

The length of the time that the child's loved one has been dead also varies, from one month to one year or more. The important point is to respond to the child's desire and readiness to participate, and to work with the parents at enrolling the children when appropriate.

Children also have repeated their participation in the next group program, which may be of some benefit to more recently bereaved children and as a method of reinforcement of the reality of their grief experience.

When circumstances of death for the children's loved ones are similar among group members, often they can be more helpful to each other and they are more willing to express their feelings. However, having all group members with similar circumstances is often not possible and this should not be a deterrent to forming the group. The facilitators will need to recognize their challenge to help each express his/her grief.

Special Needs

Special needs that the children have may warrant a referral to another agency or program. If a child is having an unusually difficult grief response, referral for further individual or family counseling is suggested. The intention of the bereavement group program is to facilitate a child's grief response, but complicated grief situations may warrant further intervention.

Children with special learning needs may require an adaptation of the activities or more individual attention in the group setting along with a follow-up intervention plan. In rare instances, screening a child out of the program who cannot gain from it may be appropriate.

REGISTRATION

Pre-registration is important in determining group size and in assessing the needs of those who are interested in attending. After the children have registered, a phone call can

Dear Children's Group Participant.

The Bellin Hospice Program is pleased that you will be joining our Children's Grief Program.

The group will be held in the Charlotte Fowler Building, Corner of Cass and Webster Avenue, Room 112. We will begin promptly at 4:00 and finish at 5:30. We invite the Parent//Guardian to participate in the first fifteen minutes of our meeting.

If you need any further information regarding the grief group please call me at 433-3683.

Sincerely,

Beth Haasl

Figure 3. Sample of a letter sent to confirm participation.

be made to each family to discuss the child's loss and the program format. A letter listing the time, place, and dates of the group sessions may be sent to confirm participation. Figure 3 is a sample letter.

PARENT/GUARDIAN COOPERATION

Parents or Guardians play an integral part in the child's grief response and need to be part of the bereavement group process. Information regarding the group objectives and activities should be shared with them to give them ideas on how to follow up at home with the child. The first session includes time at the beginning of the session to meet the parents, give a brief outline of the objectives and the sessions, and answer questions they may have.

Written information regarding a child's grief process is shared with the parents at this session. This information could include, *Talking To Children About Death*, U.S. Department of Health, Education and Welfare, National Institute Of Mental Health, 5600 Fishers Lane, Rockville, MD 20857, or the brief handout shown in Figure 4.

Suggestions to consider in implementation of a child's bereavement program are to set up a meeting with each child and their parent(s) prior to the start of the group program to discuss on an individual basis the group format and respond to their concerns, or to offer a parent's session concurrent with the children's group. This could be a facilitated group session, with the focus being on coping with their children's grief process while grieving themselves.

HELPING CHILDREN WITH THEIR GRIEF

The grieving process in children is dependent upon each child's stage of development. For instance, a three year old will experience grief much differently than a ten year old. Yet, both do experience grief. We sometimes feel that children do not understand what has happened and do not experience feelings of grief. The following is a list of suggestions to help you and your child through this grief process.

1. Discuss your feelings with your child; let them share their feelings with you. Keep your language simple; do not over explain. If you do not know the answer to one of their questions, tell them that you do not know.

2. Be honest with your child about how the death occurred. Do not use phrases such as "they are just sleeping," or "passed on," as this may confuse your child. Use the words "died and dead."

3. Read books on children's grief and the adult mourning process. This will help you to understand the grief process and how to respond to your child's needs.

4. Allow your child to go to the cemetery if they wish, or to other places where the memory of the loved one is present for your child.

5. If you are concerned that your child may be having some abnormal grief reactions, seek professional help.

Figure 4. An example of a handout for parents.

5

FACILITIES

Facilities are very important. Having space in a building that is convenient for all is essential. The space must be reserved for the specific meeting days and hours. Equipment beyond what is usually found in a meeting room or classroom is minimal.

LOCATION/SPACE

Use a group meeting room that is conducive to setting up a comfortable atmosphere for the participants. Light and space should be adequate; tables and chairs should be movable. Some activities require work space at a table, some activities involve writing at the chalkboard, and some activities, such as the puppet show, require open space; thus, a room that can be changed to adapt to the particular group needs works best.

Depending on group size and makeup, as discussed in Section IV, a second meeting room may be needed for those groups that are divided into two sections. This room will have the same needs as those discussed in the prior paragraph.

Privacy is essential for running the group. The room(s) used must be free from interruptions and prevent the conversation from being overheard by others.

Another useful suggestion is to have a lounge or separate room available for parents/guardians of the group participants who choose to wait for their children during the group, where informal sharing between them can safely occur.

Session Four may be conducted at a funeral home, in order to tour the funeral home and foster the participant's sharing of his/her funeral experience. The funeral director with whom you work needs to be comfortable with the children and have an understanding of a child's grief response. If meeting at the funeral home is not feasible for this session, the funeral director is invited to the group meeting location to share with the group about the funeral process.

Where several agencies are working together to offer a children's bereavement group program, the agencies may rotate the responsibility for acquiring adequate facilities, or they may agree to meet at the agency that offers the best facilities. If agencies are in competition with each other, meeting at a neutral location may work best, such as a church, school, or funeral home, so that one agency does not appear to dominate, to the detriment of other agencies involved.

EQUIPMENT

The materials needed for the activities in each group session are listed with the session outline. A chalkboard or flipchart to write on is helpful to have for several of the activities, along with movable table and chairs. A convenient, but not essential suggestion, is to have kitchenette facilities readily available for snack storage and preparation.

The two books that are used are the *Leader Manual* and the *Participant Workbook*. Each leader/facilitator will need a copy of the *Leader Manual*. Each participant will need a copy of the *Participant Workbook*.

Participant Workbook. The workbook presents the goals and activities for participants in a Children's Bereavement Support Group Program. The Leader Manual for *Bereavement Support Group Program for Children* provides information on conducting the group.

The *Participant Workbook* contains basic information on the topic for each of the sessions that is helpful for participants to see in written form and to be able to keep for future reference. A suggested bibliography accompanies each session which you as leader may want to supplement according to books in your local library.

The Workbook also contains worksheets for each activity that the children are asked to complete. The Workbook is intended to be theirs to keep and they may take it with them which will serve as a reminder of their participation in the group sessions.

The use of the Participant Workbook can increase communication between the parents/guardian and the children involved in the group, as they may take their works home with them between sessions and keep them when the program sessions are completed. It also may improve the children's comfort level in the group sessions, as they are able to look ahead at each of the session's activities to see what the future sessions will entail.

6

LEADERS/
FACILITATORS

Potential leaders/facilitators need to review their responsibilities, personal characteristics, and time commitment to fully understand what is expected. The rewards of helping children is great; however, if one is unable to follow-through, difficulty will result not only for facilitators but also for children and their parents.

RESPONSIBILITIES

Number of Facilitators

To have two group leaders who work well together is very important. Children's activities and needs require the attention of two adult group co-leaders in order to prevent unnecessary disturbances. It might be beneficial to enlist the services of a bereaved young person to serve as a group assistant. This assistant's loss should not have been recent, and they should show signs of recovery from that loss.

Determination of Responsibilities

Co-leaders should meet prior to the group time to review the group sessions and determine each leader's responsibilities. Agreement by the co-leaders should be reached on how to handle disturbances in the group when they arise. Ground rules, which are suggested in the description of Session One, are very helpful in keeping the group on task.

Preparation

In explaining the group activities, clear instructions geared to the age-level of the group should be given. Having all the materials available and prepared in advance facilitates the successful completion of the activities. The materials required for each activity are listed with the outline of the sessions, and to keep them in a separate storage container is convenient.

Role Model

A key role of facilitators is to provide an appropriate role model for participants. When children are sharing their grief, the facilitator should respond in an empathetic and accepting manner. Often a helpful procedure is to share with the children that they may cry while talking about their grief. Sharing brief personal examples during the activities will help participants learn how to share their grief experiences in an appropriate way.

PERSONAL CHARACTERISTICS

The following characteristics are desirable for a facilitator of a bereavement group for children.

Comfort With and Interest In Children.

The facilitator should be familiar with the developmental stages of children in order to have an understanding of the demands a child places on the group leaders and to have an awareness and sensitivity to the children's needs. Further information on child development can be obtained from various books, such as *Child Behavior*, by Frances Ilg and Louise Bates Ames, Harper and Row Publishing.

Comfort With and Knowledge of the Grief Process

The group leaders must have a general awareness of what to expect in a normal grief process. Participation in workshops on the grieving process can help expand leader's awareness of grief issues. The leader also needs to understand and have dealt with personal grief feelings and experiences, and to be aware of how they are affecting one's own work with bereaved children.

Empathy, Sensitivity, and Warmth

Children respond more to people who are open, caring, and patient, and who are genuinely interested in their thoughts and feelings. Children in grief often have difficulty in expressing their feelings, and the facilitators need to show a genuine desire to understand, listen, and respond to their needs.

Nonjudgmental Attitude

Co-facilitators need to convey an accepting attitude to participants. Open communication and expression of grief will only occur in an atmosphere where the child feels nonthreatened and totally accepted.

Flexibility

Above all, group co-leaders must be flexible in conducting the group. Depending on the makeup of the group, the suggested program format may need to be adapted. A helpful procedure to have formulated an alternative group activity for each session that can be substituted in the event that the planned activity does not meet the group's needs.

TIME COMMITMENT

A considerable commitment needs to be made on the part of each co-leader who chooses to facilitate the children's bereavement group program. The initial establishment of the group may require several months, in working with other agencies, organizing the logistics of running the group, recruiting the group members, deciding on group activities, and collecting the materials needed.

Facilitating the group's sessions also requires a significant amount of energy and commitment. Working with children is energizing, but can also be tiring. In addition, needs of the children and their parents/guardians may require attention outside of the group time, and the facilitators need to be accessible for them.

7

CHILDREN'S GRIEF REACTIONS AND CAREGIVER TECHNIQUES

The following 13 common grief responses are experienced by children. A child may have one or more of these grief responses. Following each grief response is summarized caregiver techniques that have been found to be helpful.

SHOCK/DENIAL/NUMBNESS

Immediately following the death of a loved one, the child may experience shock and disbelief; the loss does not seem real or possible. This time of feeling shocked can last only a short time or extend over several months, the average being from 6 to 8 weeks.

Caregiver Techniques.

As caregivers and parents of children we need to support the naturalness of this temporary protective mechanism, which is an important step in coping with grief. We want to help children to move towards grief, not away from it. We do this by helping them to express their feelings and to accept those feelings as a natural process that occurs after a loved one has died. The expression of feelings to others is the mourning process. Both grief (the internalizing process) and mourning (the public expression) are important.

INDIFFERENCE

At times children may seem indifferent to the death that has occurred. Their feelings of grief may be too much to accept at the present, and they may be emotionally "shut down" for a period of time. Do not mistake this indifference for a lack in feelings of grief.

Caregiver Techniques.

Help the child to become aware that this feeling is acceptable and normal, and that he or she may cry later when he or she is better able to express the feelings.

PHYSIOLOGICAL CHANGES

Children may experience physiological symptoms due to their grief. These may include some or all of the following:

> fatigue,
> difficulty in sleeping,
> loss of or an increase in appetite,
> sore throats,
> shortness of breath,
> muscle twitching (this will result in difficulty sitting still),
> headaches,
> stomach aches,
> loss of muscle strength,
> clumsiness, and
> rashes.

Children may begin to associate some of these symptoms with the ones their loved one had, which can cause children to become distressed, and to think they may be going to die also.

Caregiver Techniques

Consultation with the child's physician would be helpful when this occurs so that they can be reassured that sometimes feeling sick is part of grieving. Discussions with children regarding these changes need to occur so as to provide children with opportunities to grieve in other ways rather than just physically.

REGRESSION

Children may regress and become overly dependent. They can exhibit a desire to be cuddled and sleep with their parents. Separation from the primary care provider will become difficult, and sometimes children will throw a temper tantrum when their parent leaves the home or the room. Children may develop difficulty with staying on task, may have problems working independently, and may develop dependent seeking behaviors, such as "baby talk." Children many times have trouble with their peer relationships.

Caregiver Techniques

During this time of grief, children will seek out and be happiest with relationships that provide them with nurturing. Do not, however, reinforce regressive behaviors. Discuss them and help the child to develop adequate outside support systems so that they are better able to cope with feelings of grief by talking about their sadness, and not acting it out with regressive behaviors. Prolonged regressive behaviors are an indication that emotional needs are not being met in a healthy manner, or it may be feeding the adult's need to care for someone so that their pain is diminished. Intervention is needed if these regressive and overly dependent behaviors persist.

ACTING AS AN ADULT

At times children will try to take the place of the loved one who died. If the father has died, the oldest son may feel he needs to fill the role of father/husband within the family. The same would follow with the mother dying, with the oldest daughter trying to fill the role of being the mother/wife. This also can pose a problem for siblings. If only two children are in the family and one of the children dies, the demands that are felt by the surviving child can be great.

Caregiver Techniques

In these instances, children need to be reminded of what their role is within the family: they are not adults, do not need to take on the role of an adult, or do not need to fill the role of the deceased sibling. Children need opportunities to identify and discuss these changes in their families, and their feelings regarding these changes.

DISORGANIZATION AND PANIC

A feeling of being disorganized and out of touch with the normal proceedings of life is a feeling that many children have. Children can become afraid of the length and intensity of their feelings, and they may become concerned that they are never going to be "normal" again. Dreams, restlessness, irritability, anxiety, and the inability to concentrate may occur. Children may cry easily, and often over unrelated occurrences or nothing at all. The appearances may be that they are very unhappy, depressed, and moody.

Caregiver Techniques

These feelings need to be addressed and help needs to be given to children so they may understand that feeling these feelings is normal. Make them aware that time will be needed, and in taking time and working through the grief, things will get better. This may be a good time to discuss happy memories of the person who has died.

EXPLOSIVE EMOTIONS

Problems with self-esteem may occur for grieving children. They may feel that they are to blame for the death, or that others may have caused their loved one to die. Children often will review past times when they may have been upset with their loved one. They can view these times when their loved one was angry with them as causing the illness or accident to happen. Children can become resentful of others who they feel may have caused the death, which they may show by lashing out at the person with whom they are angry. These feelings of anger and resentment can cause the child to have explosive emotions. They will seem to just "blow up" with anger sometimes for the very smallest reasons. These emotions can cause children to feel very unhappy about themselves. Feelings of guilt and blame cause their self-esteem to lower, which may cause even more lashing out as they attempt to re-build their own self-esteem by bringing others' self-esteem down.

Caregiver Techniques

Try not to induce feelings of guilt over these explosive emotions as these feelings need to be expressed, but in a less harmful way. Discuss with the child how they might find alternative methods to express these feelings of anger and resentment.

ACTING OUT

Acting out behaviors are part of a child's grief response. Some children do feel deprived due to the death of a loved one. They may feel angry, and their response may be fighting and being mischievous which defies authority. Defying authority may be a way of keeping them from being abandoned again. They may alienate adults by acting badly, which they are doing as a way of protecting themselves from being hurt again by a loved one dying.

Caregiver Techniques

Helping children to understand why they may be having outbursts is the way to handle these situations. Children may be asking for limits on what behaviors are acceptable and try to seek out those people who really do care for them as much as the one who died.

FEAR

Children can become fearful of others dying, and they may worry that no one will be available to take care of them. These fears can lead to the dependent behavior that was presented in a previous paragraph. Children may become fearful of their own death or just fear death in general. Grief that adults around the child are expressing can also frighten the child. Children may have never seen their parents or grandparents cry before, and this can be unsettling for children. This is often why children hesitate to discuss their own grief, as they do not want to make their loved one sad and see them cry.

Caregiver Techniques

Because of fear of death and perhaps violence, this is a good time to limit television programs with violence as this may serve only to accentuate this problem.

Caregivers need to reassure the child that others always will be available to care for them. If children ask questions about death, we need to accept and answer these questions honestly. If we do not know the answer, we need to be honest and say that we do not know. Children need to be provided with extra warmth, acceptance, and understanding in order that we may dissuade their fears.

GUILT AND SELF BLAME

Children may think that wishful thoughts can lead to death. If they had wished at one time that the person who died would "just drop dead" and this person dies, this leads to feelings of guilt for the child. The child may come to view his or her past behavior as contributing to the death of the loved one. This will be more common in families who always have someone to blame for things that do not go right.

Caregiver Techniques

Reinforce and provide opportunities for the child to talk in a realistic way about how people die, and that we cannot "wish" someone to die. Children need to understand that anger is part of all relationships.

RELIEF

The feeling of relief after a long illness is a common way for adults and children to feel. In the case of a sudden death, relief that their loved one did not suffer is also common.

Caregiver Techniques

We can help children to understand that feeling relieved is acceptable and normal by anticipating that they will feel this and discussing it openly. Adults can talk about the fact that they know that sometimes we are glad that our loved ones do not hurt any more.

LOSS, EMPTINESS, AND SADNESS

Loss, emptiness, and sadness occurs when children come to understand fully that their loved one is not coming back. They come to realize this when their loved one is not there for those special times that families get together. You may see children crying more at this time than right after the death. The child may demonstrate a lack of interest in others or self, and go through withdrawal. They may have appetite and sleep changes, or be nervous.

Caregiver Techniques

Allow children to express these feelings, review the relationship with them and talk about how the person died. Even though the adult's grief may be triggered by these discussions, they need to be able to not have to shut the child off to protect themselves. If the adult is having a difficult time reliving this, seek out a support group that deals with children's grief or other professional supports. One could encourage children to write about their experience during this time.

INTEGRATION

We need to help children towards integrating their death experience. This does not mean that all is well and back to normal. Children who have integrated and healed are able to share memories and talk of their loved one easily. They may always express sorrow and anger over their loved one being dead, but they have moved on. This is a time when they are saying "goodbye" to their loved one.

Caregiver Techniques

This may require that we be more sensitive to them and their feelings. Help them return to regular eating habits, renewed energy, increased ability to think, and the ability to establish new and healthy relationships.

8

SKILLS EFFECTIVE
IN GRIEF COUNSELING

The following four care-giving skills are excellent tools to use in counseling and supporting a grieving child:

1. *Perceive*—We need to perceive that children do grieve.

2. *Understand*—The feelings of grief are a difficult task for adults to understand, and to recognize how much more we need to help and direct a child through their grieving time.

3. *Respond*—Once we see and understand the feelings, we need to respond to the feelings with honesty, warmth, acceptance, and a nonjudgmental attitude.

4. *Express*—We can help children to express their feelings if we are willing to share our own. We, as adults, are the role models. We can help children to express feelings of grief through talking, writing, and drawing about them.

Facilitators should be familiar with basic grief counseling techniques. Further information is available in *Helping Children Cope With Grief*, by Alan Wolfelt.

CREATING AN ATMOSPHERE
OF ACCEPTANCE

In order for children to share and gain from the grief group experience, an atmosphere must be present that encourages children to participate and ask questions. Facilitators must show a genuine respect for children and their concerns, and respond to each statement or question in a caring, honest, sensitive way. Only when children feel secure and comfortable will they share and ask questions openly. The children may repeat their stories or questions, and this is an appropriate way for children to be working through their grief.

Facilitators need to establish firmly with the group that no laughing or teasing about other's questions or statements is to be allowed. As the peer group response is very important to children, the atmosphere needs to be established as safe, where all questions are acceptable.

ATTENDING AND LISTENING SKILLS

Facilitators need to practice attending behaviors that will encourage children's expression of thoughts or feelings and demonstrate acceptance and respect. Eye contact, body positioning, and posture should show attention to the group and the individual members. Facial expression and tone of voice should be relaxed and reflect the emotional tone of the situation, and communicate warmth and sensitivity to children.

Listening to children who are grieving and mourning requires special skill in order to hear not only the content of what is being said, but in hearing thoughts and feelings behind their statements and the content that is only being hinted at. This takes a great deal of patience, and children may have difficulty putting their thoughts or feelings into words. If, as the facilitator, you find that you are "talking at" the children or "putting words in their mouth," in an attempt to get at their feelings, you may be trying to move the children too quickly through their experience with grief and not responding at the child's pace.

MODELING

The group co-leaders need to demonstrate to children appropriate ways of responding to grief. Talking in a relaxed, calm manner, using the words "dead, died, and grief," shows children that an acceptable procedure is to be open and to talk about death. When a child becomes tearful or cries in the session, be supportive and responsive to that child, letting the group know that sadness and tears are a natural and an appropriate way of experiencing our grief and of working through the mourning process. One of the co-leaders may be helpful to children in the group by sharing, very briefly, some personal examples of grief experiences, as long as it it pertinent to the group session and not reflecting the facilitator's own need to work through a prior loss experience.

UNDERSTANDING

Facilitators must be able to convey to children an empathetic understanding of each child's thoughts and feelings. Even when it is difficult to totally understand what the child is attempting to communicate, a desire to fully understand, and an accepting and nonjudgmental attitude will show the child that the facilitator is a caring, trustworthy adult.

AIDING THE CHILDREN
IN EXPERIENCING GRIEF

Some children have difficulty in expressing their grief, even when group leaders demonstrate good listening skills and are sensitive to and understanding of the child. The facilitator must then seek out ways to help the children to express their grief, perhaps in alternative mediums if not verbally. By using the suggested diverse activities, the facilitator can show the children ways of expressing their grief that are easier for the child. An activity, such as drawing a picture or writing a letter, also may initiate further verbal expression by the child as the activities are shared and discussed in the group.

PART B
SESSION OUTLINES
FOR
BASIC PROGRAM

SESSION OUTLINES FOR BASIC PROGRAM

The basic program consists of five sessions, each one and one-half hours in length. The length of time for each session may vary, depending on the group makeup, and the activities can be adjusted to meet time demands. The sessions must keep moving, and to do so will necessitate having a variety of activities to prevent boredom. The final fifteen minutes of each session is reserved for a snack, a time for the children to unwind from the group.

Age appropriate books that contain information on the grief process need to be made available to be checked out by the children throughout the sessions. Suggestions for appropriate books can be found in the bibliography section and are included in the *Participant Workbook* outline of each session.

Session I
INTRODUCTION AND DISCUSSION
OF DEATH/GRIEF

PURPOSES

1. To familiarize the participants with the grief group experience.

2. To establish the group rules.

3. To offer each participant an opportunity to share their death experience.

4. To hear other children's experience with death, and know they are not alone in having a loved one die.

5. To explore the children's perception of death/grief in an alternative form.

MATERIALS NEEDED

1. Participant Workbook
2. Chalkboard
3. Construction paper
4. Colored markers/colored pencils/crayons
5. Pencils

ACTIVITIES

1. Introduction to Group Sessions

Begin with a general introduction to the group program. Include an introduction of facilitators, the purpose of the program, a brief description of each session, ground rules, and general housekeeping information. Some suggested ground rules are the following five:

a. One person speaks at a time.

b. Each person has a chance to talk.

c. No one is pushed to talk.

d. No one laughs or makes fun at what someone else says.

e. What is said in the group, stays in the group.

Parents are invited to participate in this portion of the session only, and they may ask questions or voice concerns at this time. Some of the parents may choose to spend their time during the remainder of the session with other parents with whom sharing of their grief experience may occur. If possible and highly recommended, have a room available for parents to facilitate such sharing.

2. Warm-up Activity

Have participants do an activity to help them know each other and feel more comfortable in the group. Choose one of the following activities:

a. Have each participant pair up with another group member, preferably one he or she does not know. Give them five to ten minutes to interview their partner about where they attend school, what grade they are in, their family, and several interests they have. Ask each participant to introduce their partner to the full group, including the above information. This exercise works well in the first session.

b. Ask each participant to make a list of what they feel are their positive points, and then choose one to share with the group.

c. On small note cards, print a feeling on each card. Ask each participant to randomly select a card and describe a situation when someone might have had that feeling. Encourage the children to be creative!

d. An activity that is helpful as an icebreaker, especially with younger children, is to have play dough available on the table as the children arrive. They can spend the time that participants are gathering in this playful activity.

e. Give each child an opportunity to think about memories of their loved one. Ask them to share with the group a memory that he or she would like to forget and one that he or she would like to cherish.

Note: You may use one of these warm-up activities at the beginning of subsequent sessions.

3. Sharing Death Experience

Ask each participant to share information about their death experience, including who died, mode of death, how long ago the death occurred, and any other information they desire to share. This plays an important part in the group session as it helps them to confront the reality of the death, and gives them an opportunity to share about death in a safe setting.

4. Picture of Life/Death

Have the children choose a piece of colored construction paper and provide markers or crayons. Ask the children to draw their picture of death on one side of the paper, and their picture of life on the other. Figures 5, 6, and 7 are samples. This provides an opportunity for them to express their ideas on death in an alternative form, and helps them to focus on their perception of death. Allow time to have the participants share their pictures with the group. Refer to *The Art of Grief*, by Mary Raymer, ACSW, and Barbara Betker McIntyre, Art Therapist, for information on children's drawing of death.

5. Grief Letter

Briefly discuss what grief is as part of this activity. Help children to understand the benefit from expressing and sharing (the mourning process) the grief. Ask each participant to write a letter describing his/her grief to a best friend. This activity is more appropriate for use with children eight years and older, but can be used with younger children by having the group leaders assist the children in writing their letters or, if a tape recorder is available, having them speak their letters into a mike. After the participants have completed their letters, they or the group leaders can read the letters aloud if the children agree to having them shared. This again provides an opportunity to express grief in an alternative form. This is a good time to talk about the use of writing as a mourning process to assist them in working out their grief feelings.

Examples of letters written by children to express their grief are shown in Figures 8, 9, and 10. These are for illustration only and are not for distribution to children.

6. Snack

Have participants share in juice or pop and a snack of popcorn or cookies, which offers an opportunity for informal sharing and a wind-down from the session.

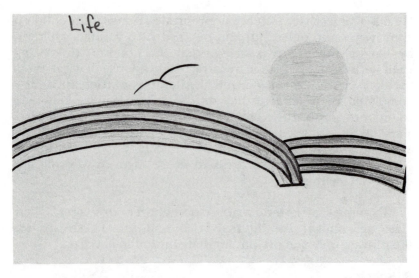

Life—Rainbow picture. 14 year old girl—her best friend died in a car accident. Children may often use birds or rainbows in their pictures of life.

Death—car accident. 14 year old girl—her best friend died in a car accident. Children may often draw from their experience with death.

Figure 5. Contrast of life and death through art.

Life—girl and boy holding hands. 8 year old girl—her only brother died by suicide. The girl and her brother were very good friends and played together often.

Death—Angel picture. 13 year old girl whose dad died of cancer. This girl's dad was sick for some time. The family was aware that death would occur.

Figure 6. Art samples reflecting life and death.

Life—two boys playing football. 7 year old boy. His brother died in a car accident. This picture of life is showing the two of them playing football.

Death—coffin picture. 10 year old boy whose brother died in a car accident. This is a picture of his brother's funeral and he is feeling sad.

Figure 7. Illustrations of how children's feelings about life and death are expressed through art.

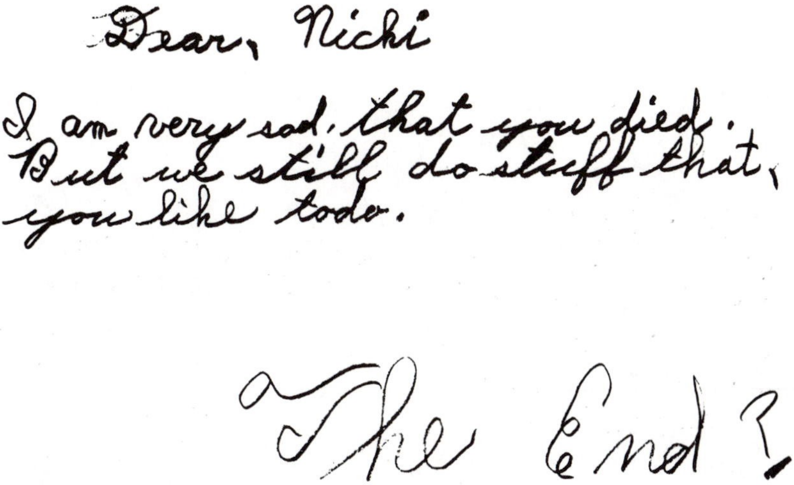

Dear, Nicki

I am very sad, that you died. But we still do stuff that, you like todo.

The End?

Nicki—14 year old girl whose best friend died in a car accident. She attended group with another friend who was also friends with the girl who died.

Figure 8. Sample of a grief letter.

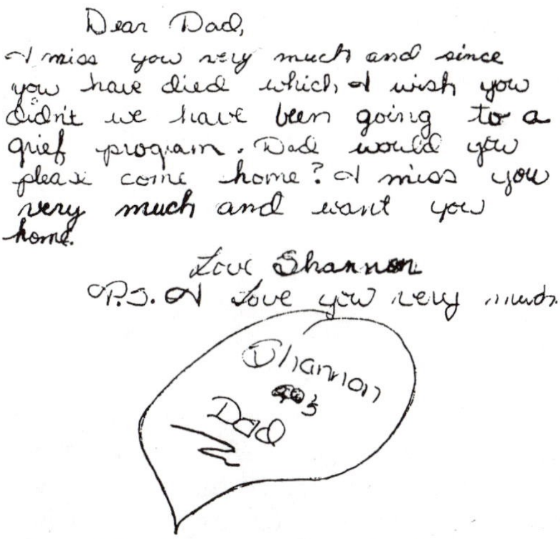

Dear Dad,
I miss you very much and since you have died which, I wish you didn't we have been going to a grief program. Dad would you please come home? I miss you very much and want you home.
Love Shannon
P.S. I love you very much.

Dad—9 year old girl whose father died in a motorcycle accident.

Figure 9. Grief expressed in a letter.

Dear Uncle Jeff

I really liked to play with Uncle
Jeff. I liked to play football, baseball,
basketball, and tag with Uncle Jeff.
I would like it if some one else
could be just like Uncle Jeff.
I would like for my soon to
be step dad, ten of my friends
named Eric, Brian, Alex, Mike, Matt,
Kevin, Matt, Dave, Jason, and J.P.
I also would like to go out
to the gravestone by myself
so I can do some praying, thinking etc.

From

Kory U.

Uncle Jeff—12 year old boy whose uncle died in a motorcycle-train accident. Kory had always been very close to his uncle and received a lot of support and positive reinforcement from him.

Figure 10. Feelings are often expressed in writing.

Session II
FEELINGS/SELF ESTEEM

PURPOSES

1. To provide information on the feelings associated with the grief process.

2. To offer an opportunity for the children to express their feelings (the mourning process) about the death of their loved one.

3. To reassure the children of the normalcy of their feelings.

4. To show a relationship between grief and self esteem.

MATERIALS NEEDED

1. Participant Workbook
2. Chalkboard
3. Colored markers/colored pencils/crayons
4. Paper plates
5. Index cards with feeling word on each

ACTIVITIES (Will need to select from the list below)

1. Warm-Up Activity

a. Have children to complete Workbook, Item 1a.
b. Have children to share positive feelings recorded in Workbook, Item 1a.
c. Distribute to each child one index card that has a feeling word on it.
d. Have each child to describe a situation when someone might have had that feeling. Encourage creativity.

2. Listing Feelings (To be done by all ages)

Ask group participants to write examples of grief feelings on a chalkboard. The children may respond more willingly if they have the opportunity to write on the board themselves. Include the following feelings:

a. sad,
b. anger,
c. guilt,
d. relief,
e. fear,
f. worry,
g. shock,
h. emptiness,
i. frustration,
j. forgetfulness,
k. numb, and
l. denial.

In talking briefly about these feelings, include these points:

a. Feelings are neither good nor bad.
b. Feelings are unique to each individual.
c. Expression of feelings can be difficult.
d. To share feelings is okay and to do so is helpful.
e. Discuss those feelings that can be part of grief.
f. Feelings of grief may be confusing and overwhelming.
g. Not everyone understands our feelings; encourage children to find persons who do.
h. Sometimes grief feelings will be shown as anger or frustration.
i. Self-esteem is affected by grief.

3. Picture of Family Grief (To be done by older children)

Ask participants to draw a picture in the *Participant Workbook* of their families and how each member is showing his or her grief. Sharing their pictures will lead the group to discuss how participants perceive members of their family deal with their grief. You may use questions such as, "Who is the saddest?" "Is anyone angry?" "Who is relieved?"

4. Feeling Picture (To be done by younger children)

Ask participants to draw a picture of a feeling in the *Participant Workbook* using markers or crayons. Read a story about feelings, such as *Little People Cry Big Tears,* by Tallie T. Miller, and Margo M. Cheney which is a good introduction to this activity. Have the participants share their pictures with the group.

5. Paper Plate Activity (For any age)

Using paper plates and markers, ask each participant to draw a face on one side of the plate showing how they feel right now. On the other side of the plate, draw a face depicting how they feel when they are grieving. Share faces with the group. Point out the following:

a. Sometimes we appear to feel differently on the outside than we feel on the inside.

b. Feelings of grief are always a part of us even though we can participate in normal activities.

c. Referring to the original list of feelings, ask the group, "How can we express these feelings appropriately? What can we do to deal with these feelings?" Group discussion can follow the sharing of ideas on how to deal with feelings in an appropriate way.

6. Guilty Feelings (For any age)

Have participants complete the sentences in their Workbook. The activity is designed to explore guilt feelings that the children may have. The children may complete their sheet individually, or they can be asked to complete the sentences written on a chalkboard, which may prompt participation. Discussion can follow about the normalcy of having feelings of guilt as a result of someone's death. Encourage children to share these feelings of guilt.

7. Snack

8. Assignment for Next Session

Remind each participant to bring a "memory object" and old magazines for the next session. The memory object should be something that reminds the child of his/her loved one who died. This could be a picture, keepsake, gift, food, or anything that shows the special significance of the relationship. Ask them to bring a magazine that can be cut up to be used for the project.

Session III
MEMORIES

PURPOSES

1. To explore the use of memories as a positive way in which to deal with grief.

2. To offer children a nonthreatening opportunity to share about their loved one.

MATERIALS NEEDED

1. Participant Workbook
2. Magazines that can be cut up
3. Large pieces of construction paper
4. Scissors
5. Paste or glue

ACTIVITIES

1. Warm-Up Activity

a. Have each child to complete Item 1a in the Workbook.
b. Have each child to complete Item 1b in the Workbook.
c. Ask children to share their memories recorded in Workbook, Items 1a and b.

2. Memory Sharing

Each participant should have brought with them a "memory object," which they share and talk about. The importance of sharing memories should be stressed during this session, even though remembering is sometimes painful. Give examples of when and how to reminisce. Reading *The Tenth Good Thing About Barney*, by Judith Viorst, may facilitate discussion here.

3. Memory Collage

Pass out a large piece of construction paper, scissors, glue or paste, and magazines. Ask participants to find pictures in magazines of things that serve as reminders of their loved ones who have died, such as foods, hobbies, interests. Have them cut out the pictures and paste them on the construction paper to form a collage. After they have completed their collage, ask participants to share them with the group.

4. Snack

Session IV
FUNERAL PROCESS

PURPOSES

1. To offer the children an opportunity to talk about their loved one's funeral.

2. To be able to explore the funeral process and ask questions of the funeral director.

3. To offer participants an opportunity to visit a funeral home when not overwhelmed with the actual funeral events.

MATERIALS NEEDED

1. Participant Workbook
2. Felt board and felt cutout figures
3. Markers
4. Sentence completion cards

ACTIVITIES

1. Picture of The Funeral

Ask the participants to draw a picture of a funeral in the Workbook. Have them share their pictures with the group. This will lead to a discussion of their loved one's funeral. Figures 11 and 12 are samples of drawings by participants.

For younger children, you may use pre-drawn pictures that show objects or activities associated with funerals. Have each child share about his or her loved one's funeral.

2. Explaining Funeral Process

Invite a funeral director to talk to the group about the funeral process and answer questions the participants may

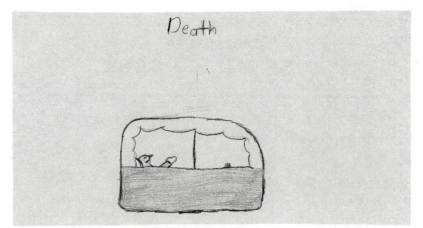

Death—man in a coffin. 10 year old boy whose father died after a long term illness. The right half of the casket was closed for the funeral, but the funeral director had opened it for this boy and his brother.

Figure 11. Memories of the funeral expressed in drawing.

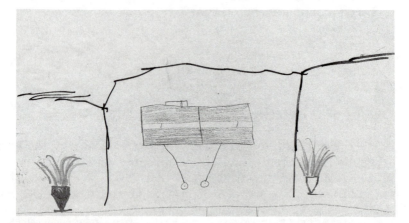

Death—Casket and plants. 13 year old boy whose brother died in a car accident. This is a picture of the casket in church.

Figure 12. Sample of a picture of the funeral as drawn by a participant.

have about funerals. Be sure to select and work with a local funeral director who is both comfortable with children and with talking about grief, in order to help children in discussing funerals.

You may do this activity by meeting at the funeral home if the group participants are receptive to this suggestion. This allows an opportunity for the children to tour the funeral home at a time when they are not overwhelmed with their own and other's grief, as usually occurs during the actual funeral. Allow the children the choice of whether to attend this session or not. Other activities may be completed in the group setting at the funeral home.

3. Felt Storyboard (To be done with younger children)

Have the younger children tell stories about their loved one's funeral, using felt boards with felt cutout figures and objects that represent things associated with funerals. Offer each child an opportunity to create a story about being at the funeral home, the funeral service, the cemetery, or the family gathering after the funeral.

4. Sentence Completion

Have the participants fill in or complete the statements in the Workbook about grief, funerals, and feelings which then can be used as a basis for discussion. Each statement also can be written on a card, which each participant chooses and then completes verbally.

5. Snack

Session V
COPING WITH GRIEF/WRAP-UP

PURPOSES

1. To express grief in an alternative way through the use of puppets and a story.

2. To offer information on constructive ways to deal with grief.

3. To review the overall program.

4. To bring closure to the group experience.

5. To encourage the children to continue sharing with their family and friends their feelings and memories of their loved one who died.

MATERIALS NEEDED

1. Participant Workbook
2. Puppets and puppet stories
3. Writing paper
4. Pencils or markers
5. Chalkboard

ACTIVITIES

1. Puppet Activities

Invite a community member who has experience performing puppet shows for children to assist you in providing a puppet show that would utilize children's stories on death. Your local librarian may have an employee or assist you in identifying a community member who works with puppets. If no one in your community specializes in presenting puppet shows, the activity can be led by the facilitators with the use of puppets, and assigning participants to work the puppets.

The following story may be used for the puppet show, or you may adapt other children's stories to meet your group needs, such as *The Tenth Good Thing About Barney*, by Judith Viorst, and *My Grandpa Died Today*, by Joan Fassler.

IT'S SAD WHEN SOMEONE DIES

One day Amy was talking with her friend, Barb. Amy's grandmother had died the week before, after a long illness.

Amy: "Sometimes I wish that people didn't die so that we could always do things that we like to do together."

Barb: "It must be sad when someone dies. If people didn't die we would all be happy. Why do people have to die anyway?"

Amy: "I don't know. My mom said that grandma was very sick and her body just stopped working, and she died."

Barb: "I guess everybody dies."

Amy: "My grandma and I used to bake cookies together, go for walks, and sing songs, and I miss doing that with her."

Barb: "Yes, I thought your grandma was lots of fun. Remember when we stayed overnight at her house and watched that funny movie and ate popcorn?" (Puppets laugh.)

Amy: "My mom said that remembering all the fun things that I did with grandma is a good way to help me feel better. But I still feel sad and cry sometimes when I'm alone in bed."

Barb: "I wonder if you'll always feel so sad that your grandma died. Doesn't it get any better?"

Amy: "My grandpa says that I'll always miss grandma and the things we did, but that after awhile I won't always feel so sad about it. He says I should talk with my mom or him when I feel sad, or do something with my friends that I like to do and that will make me feel happier."

Barb: "And maybe some day we could go visit your grandpa and sing some songs with him, or look at those pictures that your grandma showed us of when you were a baby."

Amy: "I bet he would even let us stay overnight if we wanted to. Let's go ask our moms if we can do that."

Barb: "Good idea!"

The girls go off singing together.

Following the puppet show, the puppets may be used for a role play to express feelings. Each child can suggest or be given a specific feeling or situation that he or she will act out using the puppets. The other children can guess what the feeling or situation is.

2. Constructive Ways to Deal With Grief

Ask group members to share constructive ways of coping with their grief which can be listed on a chalkboard. You might need to facilitate this discussion by suggesting some ways of coping, or reminding them of ideas previously talked about with the group. Discussion can center on the specifics of how to utilize these coping methods.

3. Letters

Ask each participant to write a letter to himself or herself describing what was enjoyed most about the group, how the experience has helped, and how he or she feels differently about the loss. This activity can introduce the idea of journaling as a way of coping with grief. These letters are then collected and are mailed back to the individuals approximately one month later, along with a personal note of thanks for participation in the group program and an expression of willingness to meet and talk more with each participant. Figures 13, 14, 15, and 16 are samples of letters written by participants.

4. Family Changes

Use the activity on changes to talk about the changes that have occurred in the family or the child's life, stressing that change is always difficult. Ask participants to complete the items in their workbooks.

5. Wrap-up with Participants

Facilitators can discuss with participants their impressions about the group and help them summarize what transpired. It may be important to point out specific things that each child did or said during the process.

6. Wrap-up With Parents

Parents are invited to attend the final fifteen minutes of this session. The facilitators can review with the parents what occurred in these sessions and elicit feedback from parents about their interactions with the children during the group program.

7. Snack

8. Remembrance

As a remembrance of the grief group experience, give each child a stuffed animal or some other momento to take home.

Dear Shannon,

   I like it because you get snacks.

The activity I liked best was when talked about feelings

Sometime you should talk with somebody about feelings. It is alright to cry.

        Bye
        Shannon

Dear Shannon—5 year old girl whose grandmother died.

Figure 13. Participant's letter to self.

Dear Jenny,

I had fun at the grief sessons we made a memory close + visited + we learned to talk to other people about our feelings and I would like to go agion

Love,
Yourself

Dear Jenny—11 year old whose sister died.

Figure 14. Letter at last group session.

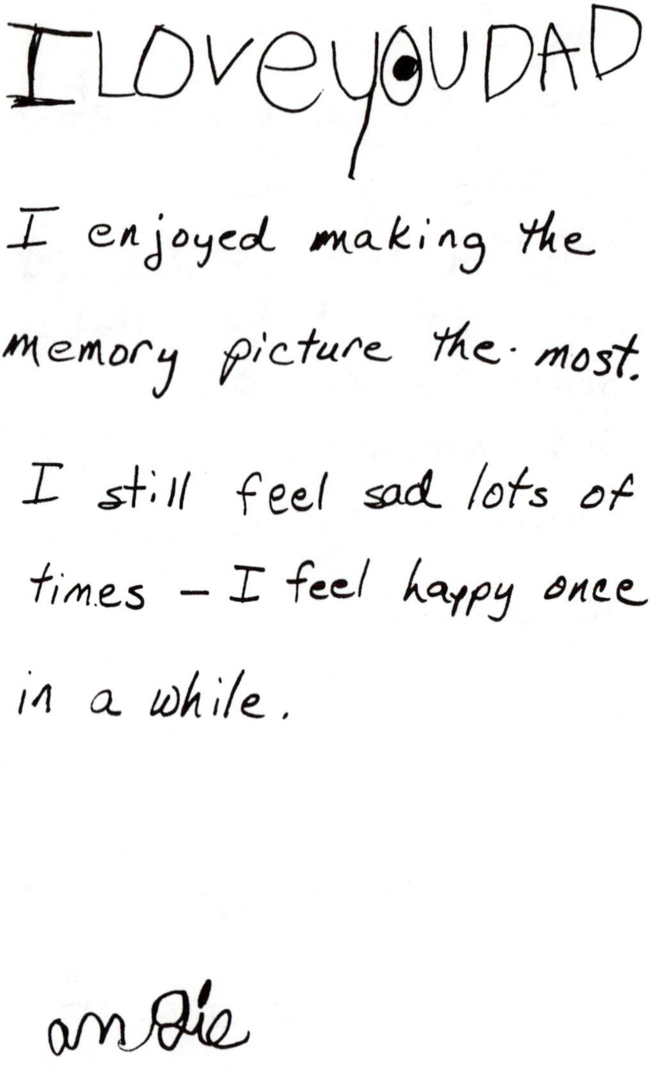

I LOVEyouDAD

I enjoyed making the memory picture the. most.

I still feel sad lots of times — I feel happy once in a while.

am<u>Q</u>ie

I love you Dad—6 year old girl whose father died in an accident.

Figure 15. Closing letter expressing feelings.

Dear Alyssa

My favorite thing to do in my grief group was making my memory collage. I also liked making my feeling faces. The feeling I made was sad and happy. I learned that grief group was fun!

Bye

Alyssa

Dear Alyssa—8 year old girl whose father died unexpectedly of a heart attack.

Figure 16. Sample letter written by a participant.

PART C
SUPPLEMENTAL
ACTIVITIES

On the following pages you will find suggested activities and topics you may want to incorporate into your children's bereavement group program. These are ideas that can be offered as additional activities, or you may design special and/or additional sessions using these activities and topics for discussion. One such time you may want to offer a special support session would be during the Christmas season, as this is generally a difficult time for children and their families.

A. MEMORY MURAL ACTIVITY

NOTE:

This activity can be used in Session III of the basic grief program, or inserted as an additional session following it.

PURPOSES

1. To facilitate discussion of favorite memories of their loved ones.

2. To allow children the opportunity to share special qualities of their loved ones.

MATERIALS NEEDED

1. Participant Workbook
2. Large piece of paper on which all participants can draw at the same time to make a mural.
3. Markers
4. Pencils

PROCEDURE

1. Ask participants to think of a special memory of their loved one who has died.

2. After they have thought of a memory, have them sketch their memory in the Workbook, or they may choose to write their memory.

3. When each participant is finished, direct him or her to find an area on the paper being used for the mural where he or she would like to draw.

4. Then from the sketch, draw on the mural paper.

5. When all have finished, display the mural on the wall.

6. Have participants take turns at explaining their memory/drawing.

B. REMEMBERING ACTIVITY

NOTE:

This activity can be incorporated into Session III of the basic program, or can be added to the Memory Mural activity as an additional session following Session III.

PURPOSES

1. To provide an opportunity for the children to think back on their relationship with their loved one who has died.

2. To facilitate the discussion of how the participants feel about their relationship with their loved one who has died.

3. To give the participants an opportunity to express desires and wishes about their relationship with their loved one who has died.

MATERIALS NEEDED

1. Participant Workbook
2. Pencils/Pens
3. Chalkboard

PROCEDURE

1. Have participants complete the following statements in their Workbooks. If the children are too young to write, read the questions, and discuss each one.

   a. The memory that I like best of my loved one is when we . . .

   b. I am glad my loved one and I got to . . .

    c. Something that has changed in my family is . . .

    d. One day I will . . .

    e. Now my family and I . . .

2. Based on your experience with the group, add other statements if you believe they would be helpful.

3. Have participants share with the group answers they wrote to their questions.

C. SAD AND/OR HAPPY FEELINGS ACTIVITY

NOTE:

This activity can be used in Session II, or incorporated into an additional session following Session II.

PURPOSES

1. To facilitate discussion of feelings.

2. To provide participants an opportunity to express their feelings in an alternative form.

3. To provide an opportunity for participants to talk about how other family members may be feeling.

MATERIALS NEEDED

1. Participant Workbook
2. Paper
3. Markers

PROCEDURE

1. Ask participants to think of a time when their family was happy.

2. Have them draw a picture of this time.

3. After they have completed this "happy drawing," ask the participants to draw a picture of a time when their families were sad. Space is provided in the Workbook.

4. Provide an opportunity for participants to talk about and share how other family members may be feeling. They may use their drawings to help them express those feelings.

D. STORY TELLING ACTIVITY

NOTE:

The activity may be used in Session V, or may be incorporated into an additional session following Session IV.

PURPOSES

1. To provide an opportunity for children to express wishful thinking.

2. To provide an opportunity for children to express feelings that are difficult to talk about, such as anger, guilt, and resentment.

MATERIALS NEEDED

1. Participant Workbook
2. Pen
3. Lined paper

PROCEDURE

1. Volunteer as one of the group facilitators to write the story as the children tell it.

2. In explaining the activity to the children, make it clear that you are writing a story about a grief experience. This activity works best after the children have participated in previous sessions dealing with grief to ensure an understanding of what grief is.

3. Ask the participants to tell how they would like to begin the story, and who the story will be about.

4. Encourage each participant to share their ideas for the story; call on children who may not feel as free in giving their thoughts.

5. Review before doing this activity what a story may be like. Figure 17 is an example of a story that was written in a children's grief group program.

THE CHRISTMAS STORY

Once upon a time there was a good Christmas! It was good because we were all together and had fun. The most fun was ripping open all our presents! The nicest gift was the go-cart, a surprise from Dad.

Christmas with Grandma was happy and sad. It was happy because it was fun. It was sad when she died. I will miss her at Christmas.

One thing I remember about Christmas with Grandma is that she made good cookies and cakes. Another thing I remember about Christmas with Grandma is that she was nice on Christmas and had fun. We love her very much.

Figure 17. An example of a story told in a Story Telling Activity.

BIBLIOGRAPHY

BIBLIOGRAPHY

Bernstein, J. (1977). *Loss.* San Francisco, CA: Seabury. A book which talks about the emotional aspects of death and grief. 10 to 17.

Boddie, C. F. (1988). *Feelings Book.* Evergreen, CO: Cordillera Co. A book that will help children and adults to express their grief emotions in alternative forms. Any age.

Brooks, J. (1973). *Uncle Mike's Boy.* New York, NY: Harper and Row. A boy copes with his sister's accidental death. 5 to 8.

Brown, M.W. (1979). *The Dead Bird.* New York, NY: Dell. A funeral for a found bird. 5 to 8.

Buscalia, L. (1982). *The Fall of Freddy the Leaf.* New York, NY: Holt, Rinehart, and Winston. Shows the life cycle through nature. Preschool to 15.

Clardy, A.F. (1984). *Dusty Was My Friend.* New York, NY: Human Sciences Press. A young boy tells a story about the death of his friend and how sharing memories can help feelings of grief. 5 to 12.

DePaola, T. (1973). *Nana Upstairs and Nana Downstairs.* New York, NY: Putnam. This is the story of a boy and his grandmother. In the story the grandmother dies and the boy tells about his feelings and how he remembers his grandmother. Preschool to 10.

Fassler, J. (1971). *My Grandpa Died Today.* New York, NY: Behavioral Publications. A story about a boy whose grandfather dies peacefully after talking with the boy about it. Preschool to 10.

Frey, D., & Carlock, C.J. (1989). *Enhancing Self Esteem, 2nd ed.* Muncie, IN: Accelerated Development, Publishers, A comprehensive review of self-esteem and contains excellent activities to assist in developing positive self-esteem. Adult resource.

Grollman, E. (1970). *Talking About Death: A Dialogue Between Parent and Child.* Boston, MA: Beacon Press. In this book you will find practical suggestions on how to talk to a child about death. Examples are provided of questions that a child might ask about death. After each question, a response and suggestions are supplied on how to answer the child's question. Adult resource.

Jackson, E. (1965). *Telling a Child About Death.* New York, NY: Hawthorne Publishing. This book deals with the developmental stages a child goes through in acquiring an understanding of death. It explains how at certain ages a child perceives and understands what death is. Adult resource.

Johnson, J., & Johnson, M. (1978). *Tell Me, Papa.* Brooklyn, NY: Centering Corporation. A grandfather tells about what happens when someone dies and about the funeral. 5 to 8.

Krementz, J. (1981). *How It Feels When a Parent Dies.* New York, NY: Knopf Publishing. A collection of short stories written by children whose parents have died. 10 to 17.

Lee, M. (1972). *Fog.* San Francisco, CA: Seabury. Growing up after a father's death. 12 to 16.

LeShan, E. (1972). *What Makes Me Feel This Way?* New York, NY: Macmillan. A book written that deals with the variety of feelings people may experience and how to understand them. 12 to 17.

LeShan, E. (1976). *Learning To Say Goodbye: When a Parent Dies.* New York, NY: Macmillan. A book written for children describing the grief they may feel and how to overcome it. 8 to 17.

Miller, T., & Cheney, M. (1972). *Little People Cry Big Tears.* Grand Junction, CO: Hilltop Hospice. This is a storybook that used nature to show a young child that crying is part of grieving. 5 to 13.

Prestine, J.S. (1987). *Someone Special Died.* Los Angeles, CA: Price/Stern/ Sloan Publishers Inc. This book does not specify who died, so it can be used with any type of death loss. It deals with angry feelings, loneliness, and remembering the loved one who has died. Adult resource.

Raymer, M., & McIntyre, B.B. (1987). *The Art of Grief.* Traverse City, MI: Grand Traverse Area Hospice. This book gives examples and explanations of how to use art as therapy for children. In this book you will find interpretations of children's art and what some symbols/pictures being drawn by children may mean. Adult resource.

Richter, E. (1986). *Losing Someone You Love: When a Brother or Sister Dies.* New York, NY: Putnam. Young people openly discuss their feelings and difficulties following a sibling's death. 13 to 17.

Rofes, E. (Ed.). (1985). *Kid's Book About Death and Dying.* New York, NY: Little Publishers. A collection of essays by children for children about death and grief. 10 to 17.

Sanford, D. (1985). *It Must Hurt A Lot.* Portland, OR: Multnomah Press. A young boy copes with his dog's death. 8 to 10.

Thornton, T. (1987). *Grandpa's Chair.* Portland, OR: Multnomah Press. A young boy uses memories to help him face his grandfather's death. 5 to 10.

Turner, A. (1976). *Houses For The Dead: Burial Customs Through The Ages.* New York, NY: McKay. Mourning beliefs and practices of many cultures discussed. 12 to 17.

Viorst, J. (1971). *The Tenth Good Thing About Barney.* New York, NY: Macmillan. A little boy remembers a pet cat that dies. 5 to 10.

Wolfelt, A. (1983). *Helping Children Cope With Grief.* Muncie, IN: Accelerated Development, Publishers. This book presents an extensive amount of information on how children grieve. It gives many examples on how to facilitate a child's grief process. In this book you will find ways to identify and understand a child's grief process, along with helpful suggestions on how to respond to and assist a child that is grieving. Adult resource.

Zoloton, C. (1974). *My Grandson Lew.* New York, NY: Harper and Row. As a boy remembers his grandfather, the memories comfort his mother. 5 to 8.

NOTES

NOTES

NOTES

ABOUT
THE
AUTHORS

BETH HAASL

Beth is a graduate of the University of Minnesota, with a Bachelor's degree in Family Social Science.

Beth is employed by Bellin Hospice as a Grief Counselor. Beth has had eleven years of experience in the field of grief counseling. She co-facilitates the Children's Bereavement Group Program at Bellin Hospice, Green Bay, Wisconsin, which she was instrumental in developing and has been successfully running for the past six years.

Beth has been involved with conducting workshops on children and grief in her community and throughout the state.

JEAN MARNOCHA

Jean graduated from the University of Wisconsin, Milwaukee, with a Master's Degree in Social Work. For her final research project, she completed a literature review of theoretical and research materials available on the topic of a child's response to the death of a parent. She has conducted workshops on children and grief throughout the state.

Jean is currently co-facilitating the Children's Bereavement Group Program at the Bellin Hospice, Green Bay, Wisconsin, which she was intrumental in developing and has been successfully facilitating for the past six years. She also works as a grief therapist in an outpatient clinic, and as an Employee Assistance Program therapist.